VICTIM TO VICTORIOUS

a 28 Day Fresh Start Program

By
EDWIGE GILBERT

Copyright © 2021 by **Edwige Gilbert**

All rights reserved. No part of this book may be used or reproduced by any means, graphic, electronic, or mechanical, including photocopying, recording, taping, or by any information storage retrieval system, without the written permission of the publisher except in the case of brief quotations embodied in critical articles and reviews.

To Diana Davis
for her dedication and compassion.

To the survivors of human trafficking,
child labor, child marriage and spiritual abuse,
for their resilience and strength.

I see you and I claim Victory to you!

Table of Contents

Acknowledgements 1
Introduction 3
Chapter 1: How Does This Book Work? 13
Chapter 2: Get Your Backpack Ready 17
Chapter 3: Meditation The Foundation For Your New Life 21
Chapter 4: Clear 25
Chapter 5: Dexxtra 45
Chapter 6: Create 53
Chapter 7: Next Step 75
Chapter 8: Looking Forward 79
Chapter 9: Signposts for Your Spiritual Journey 85
Chapter 10: Final Words 91
About Edwige Gilbert 99

Acknowledgements

First and foremost, I want to thank **Diana Davis** for encouraging me to write this book so I can assist the survivors of human trafficking, child labor, child marriage and spiritual abuse on their journey towards self-recovery and "joie de vivre".

I want to thank Emmanuel Banks who assisted me and kept me accountable on this challenging journey of writing a book.

I want to thank my friend and business partner Mike McGann for taking the time in his busy schedule to provide his magic touch with his exquisite story-telling skills.

I want to thank my Brazilian "soul daughter" Livia Maciel, for understanding how to transform my manuscript into a real book so it can be published.

I am ever so grateful to my artist friend Louis Imperato, who created a masterpiece on my book cover and who beautifully captured the meaning of the book.

I want to thank my beautiful Mother, Christiane Alter, who always believed in me, loved me unconditionally and taught me the art of Joie de vivre.

VICTIM TO VICTORIOUS

To Melanie Cabot, founder of the Palm Beach "Happiness Club," who facilitates the expression of Joie de vivre for so many including me.

To Robert Seibel my friend and lawyer who was the first to volunteer to read my early drafts and told me it was a best seller in the making.

To my spiritual Soul sister Marie-Therese Ancellin, who gave me words of wisdom and good ideas for the book.

Finally, to my special friends, Martine Legoff, Janet Lowry, Anita Lamberti, Nora Barr, Ayskel Edgerton, Anna Maria Kanga, Bonnie Roseman Christina Corbett and Stephanie Branscomb who cheered me all the way to the finishing line.

Introduction

Picture this... A little French girl in a small cabin on a cruise liner in a huge ocean, not knowing where she is, where she is going, or who the stranger taking care of her is. Trapped...

Now picture this... A young Polish man at the mercy of his enemies in a concentration camp during World War II, not knowing how to escape, or if there is a chance of surviving...only knowing his father had already died there. Trapped...

And this... A beautiful young French mother in tears, despairing, with no other choice but to leave her only beloved daughter in the care of a stranger. Trapped...

One way or another, we all know what it's like to be trapped... Trapped by our inevitable circumstances, trapped by our own destructive behaviors, and most often, trapped in mental prisons of our own making!

Thankfully the exit door is the same for us all!

Welcome to "**Victim to Victorious**, a Fresh Start in 28 days".

Deep down, you know that now is the time to reclaim your life, to make peace with your past, to release all the traumas, and heartbreaks, and to look forward to a future filled with confidence and "joie de vivre".

VICTIM TO VICTORIOUS

I am honored that you have chosen me to be your guide on this transformational journey!

What can you expect from this book?

I have designed this book as a tool kit to restore your sense of self, your emotional well-being and to experience a complete mind/body balance in just 4 weeks or 28 days.

Expect to discover:

- Thoughts to inspire you
- Meditations to motivate you
- Techniques to recondition your mind
- Strategies to create emotional balance

I have deliberately chosen the term *"tool kit"* because I want you to understand that the **"Fresh Start Program"** is easy to use and will work for you! I am confident of that because I have tested it on myself and on thousands of people from all walks of life. And the results keep coming to me, you may find them on my website: www.newlifedirections.com

> *With Edwige's FRESH START program, I was able to overcome 20 years of negative patterns, and I understood how to replace them with healthier ones that changed my life.*
>
> —MOHAND SIDI SAID, VP, PFIZER

Warning: I am not promising you a life without stress or unpleasant emotions! It would be a lie and we both know it! What I promise, is that you will find your power and you will have tools to transform your stress.

Remember that this tool kit only works if you work it by following the instructions carefully. If you have an urge to change anything, just know it is at your own risk and I decline any responsibility for the results!

Why would you listen to me?

You see, my passage into this life was difficult. I wasn't given any advantages and had to create my own victory from a victim birth. As I struggled to be born, my mother had an emergency cesarean. She wasn't expected to live but luckily, she summoned the energy to survive the trauma. I was not expected to live either; I was left oxygen deprived and placed into an incubator separated from my mother for over 2 weeks. This is known as one of the strongest traumas possible, all as I entered this world!

Yet here I am, writing this book as my victorious self and claiming it for you too! Between my instinct for survival and a dedicated nurse, I am alive to tell the story.

Not long after that my Polish father and French mother decided to leave for America to seek their fortune. However, things did not turn out the way they wanted. Between my mother who could not speak English and my father who could not find any work, there was no money to return to France. They were trapped!

The only option was to hand me over to my grandmother, who could take care of me while they searched for a way out!

They met a French nanny who was planning to go to France. She accepted to take me with her. You see, in the late 50's people would primarily travel by boat. So, at the age of just 3, this little innocent girl departed on the "Constitution", the cruise liner which used to cross the Atlantic. I have no memory of what happened on that trip, and will never know, except that I could not find my Mommy! The trauma of abandonment began there and then.

10 days later I arrived in France, picked up by my aunt who said that I looked so sick she thought I would die. I was placed in my grandmother's care and luckily, I was raised in a glamorous town named Cannes on the French Riviera, famous for its film festival each year.

My grandmother was a devout Catholic who believed that you had to suffer on this earth to be rewarded in heaven. I now see how that trapped me! Every Sunday I was forced to go to Church and confession which scared me to death. To me that was the most horrendous experience! I was in the dark, seeing only the shadow of the priest's face, hearing only his loud, punishing voice condemning me to hell! It seemed like this was already hell! I must admit that guilt and shame were the only things that I learned from this experience…that and my distrust of organized religions.

Not only was my grandmother severe, but she was also very controlling and would watch every move I made. Every time I tried to venture on my own to do something new, I would hear her disapproving voice *"Tu ne peux pas"* (You can't do it) and that would stop me. Shackled by this excessive protection, guess who I became? A creature both fearful and shy, a walking invitation for a rescue mission!

But that rescue mission was not immediately forthcoming. I grew up with these restrictions and with parents I would only see occasionally. And although I never felt them truly present in my life, in my 20's, I made the bold decision to join them. I ventured to America and landed in New York City, the "Big Apple".

I was a stranger in a strange land with my only constant companion, my grandmother's voice in my head repeating "you can't". Still trapped! I tried to escape that voice by stuffing my feelings down, and stuffing my face with bagels and brownies, not a diet I would recommend! Within 6 months I gained 30 pounds and lost every ounce of my "joie de vivre", my healthy body and my budding modeling career. I found myself overweight and brutally depressed! A victim of a trap, but this time, one I had built for myself. I found what I thought was an exit: prescription diet pills, starvation, and compulsive aerobic exercise. Of course, that was just a worse trap than the one before. Physically wrecked and spiritually empty, I knew I had to embark on a quest for a "real" exit, a freedom, lasting peace, an honest physical and emotional health.

Thankfully I can say that I made it, I found it! Victory to me!

The techniques and strategies I have discovered, a culmination of my life's work have helped me maintain my healthy weight, my emotional stability and spiritual fulfillment... in other words my "joie de vivre"!

I now present it to you because I know deep in my heart YOU CAN have it too!

What's in it for me? The gift of helping others escape their prisons is my life's purpose! And by the way, I am still a fashion model for fun today and my new constant companion is a voice that says, "I can" and that voice belongs to me!

VICTIM TO VICTORIOUS

Oh, and that mother and daughter separated by desperation, harsh circumstances, trauma, and fear are now reunited. Through my journey from "*Victim to Victorious*", my mother and I have become closer than we've ever been, and we get to celebrate our "joie de vivre" together.

In the meantime, that Polish, prison survivor father, sought his own exit. He finally found happiness. Unfortunately, he left my mother, but found his new love and got remarried to a Polish woman, moved to Sarasota Florida, and recently passed away after living a full life!

I hope I showed you what is possible in life by telling you my victim to victorious story…

Now it's your turn!!!

Are you ready to step through the exit door?

> "*Every time you are tempted to react in the same old way, ask if you want to be a prisoner of the past or a pioneer of the future.*"
>
> -DEEPAK CHOPRA

For over 30 years, I researched everything I could, related to self-help. I studied a wide variety of philosophies, psychotherapies, and mind/body regimens. On the way, I obtained certifications in Yoga, Qi Gong, Hypno-therapy, Substance abuse counseling, Neuro linguistic programming and Life Coaching.

I tested all my techniques in the "Addiction Institute of New York" an upscale 28-day substance abuse center (the counterpart of the Betty Ford Clinic) where I worked for over 20 years and which inspired me to write my first book "*The Fresh Start Promise, a total mind body spirit transformation in 28 days*".

VICTIM TO VICTORIOUS

I came to realize that the biggest mistake people make when they are looking to change their lives is to use willpower. Forcing yourself to change does not work, because the mind perceives this attempt as painful. After all, we can't forget that we are creatures of habit: our mind will do anything to keep us in our comfort zones, away from pain! What we need to do instead, is find a way to make ourselves feel good, peaceful, and safe within.

I discovered the power of belief and imagination and *"Act as if you were and you will become"* became my favorite mantra.

Right now, it may seem like the deck is stacked against you, maybe you are feeling trapped, but rejoice, you no longer need to feel like a victim and be stuck in that place! Start imagining the way your life can be and will be. Once you discard your sabotaging habits of thinking and behaving, which as you know come from childhood, you will discover that life is a journey, and that you have the freedom to choose a new empowering direction.

What to Pack for your Journey?

You'll want to travel light! No excess baggage allowed! Your backpack includes:

- An open mind.
- An open heart.
- The desire to pursue your identity
- A deep commitment to change.

Leave room for things you'll pick up along the way: food for thought, healing techniques, affirmations to open your heart. Then you will have empty space for love, trust, and vibrant energy.

VICTIM TO VICTORIOUS

Where do you begin?

Read and sign The Victory Contract. This is a very important promise to yourself, and it seals your commitment to your successful future.

VICTIM TO VICTORIOUS

FRESH START VICTORY CONTRACT

I, _____, recognize that:

- I am worthy of respect and self-respect.
- I am meant to have a rich and fulfilling life.
- I have within myself gifts, talents, strengths, and unrealized potential.
- I am willing to choose a kind and caring attitude towards myself.
- I can transform my life.

Therefore, I will:

- Be clear about my purpose.
- Be kind and loving towards myself and others.
- Look within for guidance and divine intelligence.
- Look at every challenge as an opportunity to further my dream.
- Discard outdated, counterproductive, and anxiety-producing ways of thinking.
- See myself victorious
- Be open-minded and adventurous.
- I will pursue my goals with clear intention and honesty. I am willing to do the work required to transform my attitude and my life. Nothing and no one can stop me from manifesting the person I desire to be.

I Claim my Victory Now!

_____   _____

(sign)   Date

VICTIM TO VICTORIOUS

Victory to you for signing this document! Give yourself a big hug and get ready for life change.

Chapter 1

How Does This Book Work?

As you've already learned, change becomes possible only when we understand that it is futile to willfully struggle against our habitual patterns of behavior. Instead, our focus needs to shift to rebalancing our emotions, using the power of compelling images, engaging in kind words, and inspiring thoughts, so that our minds allow us to create new, healthy behaviors.

The foundation of Making a Fresh Start program can be summed up in 3 fundamental statements **I Can! I Do! I Will!**

Each day when you wake up in the morning declare **I Can! I Do! I Will!** Anytime you encounter challenging situations you declare

I Can! I Do! I Will!

Why start with **I Can**? Because it acts to free the mind of negativity and give it permission to change. Why **I Do**? Because it ensures that you take action and create the desired change. Why **I Will**? Because it mobilizes your spirit and creates a commitment for that change to be made in 28 days or just 4 weeks. Why the number 28? Because Neuroscience has discovered the plasticity of the brain which means that new behaviors and habits can be created, and 28 days is the time needed for the brain to develop that new neural pathway and achieve your desired results.

The format of this book is straightforward: it's a two-step approach: **Clear and Create.**

In the first step **Clear**, the outcome is to:

- **Clear** non-productive habits and behaviors stopping you from being the best you can be.
- Erase self-limiting beliefs affecting your self-esteem and self- confidence.
- Discard your inner critic and negative self-talk which sabotage your attitude and state of mind.

I will first introduce you to Meditation and Mindfulness, these truly are the foundation of the **"Fresh Start Program"**

Then I will share with you quick techniques, which take only 10 minutes or less and clear non-productive emotions, like anxiety, fear, anger, sadness, and overwhelm, which stop you from accomplishing your daily tasks.

I will offer you a strategy to recondition your mind, addressing any resistance to the change that you so much desire.

You will even discover how to clear fatigue and sluggish energy and change your eating habits to ensure optimal health. Doesn't it sound like Victory to you?

Then you will be ready for step 2 **CREATE**

As with step 1, with "**Clear**" you will understand how to create a new productive habit or behavior to move you towards your vision of success. You will discover new empowering beliefs to make you feel confident, enthusiastic, and unstoppable! Finally, you will become your inner **coach** instead of your inner **critic,** gaining a new language, the language of the heart! It's a language of love and compassion towards yourself and others. And yes, YOU CAN do this!

Chapter 2

Get Your Backpack Ready

Open your mind and get ready to stretch your imagination way out there! I would like you to view your mind as a house. If you are familiar with the expression head space, you won't have too much difficulty here. Let's say you have tried to change in the past to make a better and happier life, but without much success. As a result of that experience, you feel you are cramped into an existing space which is too small, feeling suffocated, without any room to breathe and no way out.

Now it's time to renovate. Let's take a tour of your house.

First stop, the living room, this is the space of conscious awareness. This room is filled with fixtures and furniture, these are your thoughts. Notice how some of the furniture needs brighter newer fabrics, and others can be thrown out altogether. You can't relax in a cluttered space! It's in this living room that you will conduct your **Clearing** practices, where you will develop greater self-awareness and learn the language of the heart, the language of love and self-compassion.

Second stop, the basement! On one side is the "Subconscious Library" a space with many shelves, filled with the records of your life experiences including unproductive memories from the past. These are stored in your mind, and they need to be reprogrammed to free you from the effect of your past, which we will deal with later. For now, take a good look around and notice some empty shelves, waiting to be filled with positive new volumes, inspirational books of empowering and happy stories that you'll create in the space on the other side: *"The Screening Room"*.

It's empty, with just a chair in the center, facing a very large high-definition TV.

When you sit in that chair, you conduct your creative practice. You are the actor rehearsing the change you want to make. You'll imagine how you will look, what you will hear, and how it will feel to step into that joyful and successful life of yours!

Take a moment now and imagine the next 28 days of your life. Picture yourself waking every morning, opening your eyes, smiling, and declaring "I am happy to be me, and I welcome the world of infinite possibilities! Victory to Me! Victory is mine!"

This is how it is in the **"Fresh Start Program"**.

Are you excited and ready to begin the practice of change? Let's get started!

FOOD FOR THOUGHT

"Whether you believe you can or believe you can't, you are right."

-HENRY FORD

"There is nothing so disobedient as an undisciplined mind. There is nothing so obedient as a disciplined mind."

-BUDDHA

"A man who is of 'sound mind' is one who keeps the inner madman under lock and key."

-PAUL VALERY

"We are what we repeatedly do."

-ARISTOTLE

"The mind is like a clock that is constantly running down and must be wound up daily with good thoughts".

-FULTON J. SHEEN

Chapter 3

Meditation
The Foundation
For Your New Life

Are you out of your mind Edwige? Did you mean to say Medication instead of Meditation?

NO, I did not make any mistake and YES, you are right I am out of my mind, my once insane mind! Remember I was like you when I first began my journey! Meditation felt like punishment! Sitting still, doing nothing, and watching my breath?!? I was very restless, keeping myself busy all the time! Silence and self-reflection were not my idea of a good time, and by the way, have you ever wondered how you could watch your breath with your eyes closed? Total madness to me!

And the sitting assignment, forget about it! Crossed legs on a cushion, back straight, not moving a muscle! I am not a contortionist you know! And what about the battle of the voices, yelling at each other inside my head! One telling me to stay, another one to go, and one calm voice whispering in my ear, "Just give it a try!"

Through meditation, I realized for the first time that stuffing my feelings with chocolate, ice cream and cookies was not the answer to finding peace and happiness. Meditation has been my salvation, my way out of depression and my way into my safe place within.

Welcome to Meditation, the practice of self-discovery!

To realize you finally have a solution to quiet the constant mental chatter and to clear away the anxious and critical thoughts, is a relief you will soon discover as you journey through this book. To stop playing games with yourself and to honestly observe the workings of your mind - what a miracle! Your mind without proper training can be a complete nightmare! In India, they call it the *"Monkey Mind"*. It runs up and down the tree for hours! This *Monkey Mind* will take you into the past and bring you into the future without even moving a muscle. It's like space travel. It reviews yesterday, pointing out what you should have done instead, feeding you with regret and guilt. It warns you about the future, conjuring fear and doubt and it all ends up making you feel horrible, weak, victimized. And none of it is true! It's totally ridiculous! My suggestion to you: give meditation a try, it could end up being your savior! It was for me! It can be for you too!

What I have not told you yet, is that with Meditation practice there is a dramatic increase in the activity of the left side of the prefrontal neocortex of the brain associated with a sense of well-being, combined with an experience of heightened states of peace and contentment. The most practical and popular technique to achieve this result is using the breath to focus all your attention on your breath. You can count it as you feel it entering and leaving your body.

You will discover that the awareness of your breath takes you into the present moment. There is no way you can think and be aware of your breath at the same time! Conscious breathing is truly the answer to stop your mind from running in circles.

Another amazing realization about Meditation is that with long term practice, patience and persistence, your mind becomes your devoted servant, respectful and obedient, recognizing you as its master.

Whoever said that the definition of insanity is doing the same thing over and over, expecting different results, has obviously never had to reboot a computer!

I know we are all obsessed with our computers, but let's be clear on one thing: you **have** a mind, and you **are** the spirit!

Big difference! Let me explain:

Think of your **mind** as a computer! It works! But can you think of **yourself** as a computer? It does not work!

Your mind, whether you realize it or not, is the largest and most elaborate computer ever created on planet earth. Unfortunately, it doesn't come with an instruction manual, so no one really understands how to use it! Some of us are good at deleting unfortunate memories from our past. Others can save successful ones in the back of their minds, but what most of us don't know, is how to download a long-lasting program for peace and joy.

VICTIM TO VICTORIOUS

This is what I am offering you in the *"Fresh Start Program"*! Are you convinced yet? Ready to give it a try? I thought so!

Chapter 4

Clear

We are officially embarking on the Clear and Create journey, and to prepare for it I offer you some inspiration!

Meditation to Inspire You on the Journey

"The Rowboat"

HOW TO LET GO OF WORRIES

VICTIM TO VICTORIOUS

Sit comfortably and breathe deeply.

Imagine it is a sparkling summer day. You are in a boat on a peaceful lake. It could be a kayak, a canoe, a rowboat, a small sailboat, any boat you like. Have a look around. Notice all the details… the blue sky reflected on the surface of the waters… the light breeze that cools your face and gently moves the leaves of the trees on the shore. The lake is crystal clear, with a sandy bottom.

You want to take your boat out to explore the lake, but you realize it is filled with bags, boxes, and packages slowing the boat down.

Now pick up a bag filled with the anxieties of your day. Take a moment to say goodbye to them, then toss the bag overboard. What happens? Does it sink like a stone, or float away behind you?

Your boat starts to move a little faster, but it is still heavy. You realize that you have the perfect opportunity to unburden yourself further, so pick up a box of worries and throw it overboard.

You begin to move more swiftly now.

Continue to throw your concerns into the water. As you do so, your boat becomes lighter and lighter until you notice it's gliding effortlessly across the water. You breathe more peacefully and deeply taking in the clean, fresh air.

VICTIM TO VICTORIOUS

You feel the sun on your head, and you listen to the gentle sounds of the water lapping against the hull.

Doesn't it feel good to release these burdens? Don't your shoulders and neck feel looser? Aren't you more peaceful and relaxed?

Take a moment to memorize these feelings and sensation, and when you want to, head back to shore. Know that you can take your boat out anytime you like to return to this peaceful experience. The more you exercise your imagination the easier it will be for you.

Let's Begin!

This technique is very simple and can be used anytime, anywhere. I recommend you sit to start, but after 28 days you can choose what you like. I choose to practice at night lying, in bed, it helps me get rid of the "Monkey Mind"!

The Square Breathing Practice

Sit comfortably with your legs uncrossed, feet on the ground, back straight. Become aware of your breathing: start by taking a very deep breath and release that breath all the way, squeezing out every drop of air. Repeat this practice 3 times, making sure you allow your lungs and belly to fill up with air like a balloon with your inbreath, and to deflate your balloon belly with your outbreath. Now I want you to place one hand covering your navel and when you breathe in through your nose make sure you notice your belly rise and when you breathe out watch your belly fall. Keep this breathing going (called *"abdominal breathing"*) as we are getting ready to count the breath.

Ready? Start counting the breath with:

4 counts:

Breathe in 1 2 3 4. Hold the breath 1 2 3 4. Breathe out 1 2 3 4. Rest without breathing 1 2 3 4.

Now 5 counts

Breathe in 1 2 3 4 5. Hold the breath 1 2 3 4 5. Breathe out 1 2 3 4 5. Rest without breathing 1 2 3 4 5.

Last 6 counts

Breathe in 1 2 3 4 5 6. Hold the breath 1 2 3 4 5 6. Breathe out 1 2 3 4 5 6.

Rest without breathing 1 2 3 4 5 6. Breathe in again… then continue with your natural way of breathing. Take a moment to notice how you feel! More calm? focused? Now put a smile on your face, by just lifting the corners of your lips towards your ears, it's called the "Buddha smile". Your intention is to smile at this moment, expressing appreciation, gratitude for this exercise, for yourself and for your willingness to try something new! Now declare out loud: *"Victory to me! Victory is mine!"*

I hope that you begin to understand the purpose of meditation on your transformational journey, because I want to introduce you to another aspect of meditation which is known as *"Mindfulness"*. It has changed my attitude and has affected my life in such a profound way! You will see why!

Part I The state of Mindfulness

So, what is Mindfulness? Mindfulness is simply an awareness of the present moment! Unlike the traditional meditation which I told you should be practiced sitting cross legged or on a chair, Mindfulness can be practiced walking, eating, driving, at your desk or any other place you can think of! You just need to become aware of the present moment filtered through your five senses. You start with the breath, of course, then you add what you see, hear, smell, taste, and any additional sensation you may feel in your body. It is very organic! You choose to notice everything you can in that moment with one condition: no thought of any judgment. No right, wrong, good, or bad. It simply is! It has been a very liberating practice, for me since I'm French and critical by culture! Practicing Mindfulness made me a nicer, more loving person both towards myself and others, feeling much more relaxed and joyful.

The 3C's Mindfulness Meditation Experience

As the result of my training and experience in both meditation and Mindfulness practice, I have designed this practice of the "*3 C's Calm, Centered and Connected*" which incorporates both and is a vital part of the Clearing step.

The 3C's is available on my website, Newlifedirections.com

http://www.newlifedirections.com/contact.html

When you listen to it, I highly recommend you use earphones, so that it can directly access your subconscious mind, where long lasting change takes place.

For this meditation to work, it must be done every day, once in the morning and once again at night. Remember practice may not make it perfect but the words will become familiar to you, so that by the end of the 28 days, you won't need to read or to hear it any longer, it will have been recorded inside your head, and will become a new positive recording to add to your *"subconscious library"*!

Are you ready to give it a shot? YOU CAN do this!

Sit up in your chair now, straightening up your spine, putting your feet on the ground. Exhale 3 times through your mouth to cleanse and release your stress.

Now, imagine a golden string pulling you up, connecting your head to the blue sky - the world of infinite possibilities. Imagine roots growing from your feet, or powerful magnets locking your feet to the ground, connecting you to Mother Earth - securing and nurturing.

Notice your breathing. Give your full attention to breathing OUT all the worries and concerns of your day. Place a hand on your belly and notice what happens. Feel your hand going down as you exhale, and then rising as you inhale. Notice the continuous flowing motion, as your exhalation becomes your inhalation. Allow yourself to drift into a quiet calmness inside.

Continue to repeat **"let go"** with the out breath... **"Calm"** with the in breath... '**let go**... **"Calm"** begin to notice that your breath is slowing down more and more, helping you feel more and more relaxed. Give yourself permission to release anything that you feel is in the way of this calming experience. As you breathe out, say to yourself **"LET GO"** as you breathe in say to yourself **"CALM"**.

CALM. My mind is like the silent bottom of the sea. No ripples of thought disturb it.

CENTERED. I breathe and gather all my energy back into my belly, my sacred power center.

CONNECTED. I am surrounded by a circle of pure light from the sun.

This life force connects me to the world of infinite possibilities.

Before you return observe and experience the balance of energies between the left and right sides of your body. Notice and enjoy its perfect symmetry.

Remember by your daily practice of the 3C's you are creating a connection to yourself, a place to take refuge in when you feel unsafe in the outside world. It's your safe place within, which will never let you down. To access it quickly just use these words... "**Calm... Centered... Connected.**"

These words are your personal combination. Repeated over time, they will recondition your mind and your mind's responses. These words will unlock the door to peace. You can use them any place and any time you need to return to emotional balance, in the car, on the plane or in line at the supermarket. "**Calm... Centered... Connected.**"

Practice the 3Cs, taking deep calming breaths and begin to use this word combination:

"Calm, Centered, and Connected." From a place of balance and calm, all possibilities, actions and emotions become open to you now.

Part II Mindful Experiences

So far on our journey, we have covered a basic Meditation, a Mindfulness Meditation with *the 3C's*, and now, I feel you are ready to experience two very practical examples of Mindfulness practice.

The first one will be conducted outdoors and the other one will be performed eating at home or in a restaurant.

The Mindful Walk Practice

Walking mindfully is a practice which originated in the Far East. It is used as a form of meditation, one that helps establish awareness, and creates a clear and calm state of mind.

I first witnessed this on a visit to Thailand. I was spending the day at a Buddhist temple, meditating, and exploring the grounds and surrounding countryside. At one point in the afternoon, I spotted a bald monk wearing a saffron robe, walking through the gardens, but walking in a way I had never seen before, a way I could never forget: he was moving slowly, totally focused, fully aware and engaged in the simple act of walking. Simply by placing one foot in front of the other, he seemed to be at absolute peace with himself and his environment. He was serene, filled with reverence. All I could do was to simply watch, amazed, as this monk made his way through the gardens in a state of absolute awareness and grace.

It wasn't until a year later when I had the very good fortune to attend a talk by Thich Nhat Hanh, the Buddhist master, teacher, and poet that I understood what I had witnessed on that remarkable day at the Thai temple, explaining the mindfulness walking technique that had so entranced me. Thich Nhat Hanh provided the following instruction:

"When you walk, think that you are kissing the earth with your feet and that you are touching the sky with your eyes." What an exquisite metaphor! What a simple, yet exact description of what I had seen that day.

So, are you ready now for this new experience? Then let's take a walk!

Ask yourself: Where am I? what do I see? Look around, as you walk slowly and steadily. Take all the time you need, to become present to your experience! Breathe deeply and notice how the air tickles your nostrils. Each time you breathe, notice how cool the air feels tickling your nose. Continue the walk, paying attention to the presence of your feet, from the way they touch the ground, to your pace, and while you still see what you see with fresh eyes, notice any scent in the air. I hope, by now, you are getting the gist of this experience! Far from being boring, right? Pay attention to what your arms are doing and whether your hands are gripping or letting go. You can choose, if you like, to send a message to your hands, and simply think to yourself the word: *"Relax"*

Now let's switch the focus of attention to what you hear!

Birds, the sound of the ocean, people talking in the distance. Maybe the sound of silence? I am serious, there is one! You don't hear it? Try harder! I am just joking. :-)

Think to yourself and repeat the Buddhist monk's words: "As you breathe in, calm your mind and your body, and as you breathe out, smile at this moment, which is *the "only moment here now, now here"*. I hope you have enjoyed this experience and that you realize that you don't have to be a monk to walk like this. Just carry with you Thich Nhat Hanh's evocative instructions and remember that the secret to enjoying it is to suspend any judgement! The more you practice, the better you feel, and it all happens effortlessly! It's so simple and yet so powerful!! Not forcing anything, but flowing **with** everything, it's the pathway to a wonderful life.

Mindful Eating

> FOOD FOR THOUGHT
>
> *"To eat good food keeps the body in good health, it is a duty. Otherwise, we shall not be able to keep our mind strong and clear".*
>
> -BUDDHA

Have you heard about the man who finished his 14 days diet in 3 hours and 12 minutes?

I don't know about you but in my twenties I had so many issues with my weight! I was totally obsessed with it, and incapable of maintaining it! I was constantly on a diet and working out like a maniac, with the hope I'd lose those extra pounds!

I concluded that the more I stayed focused on losing the weight, the bigger I got. At the time, it didn't make sense to me the way it does now: The issue is never the weight, the issue is the emptiness inside, and the unhealthy habits that come along with it. If you want to change, you need to find a way to make yourself feel good and practice mindful eating! I  know, it sounds strange, but I promise, it is going to make sense to you!

Let me ask you this: do you finish a bag of chips or an entire pint of ice cream without realizing it? Do you chew and swallow food without noticing it? Do always crave something even if you are not truly hungry. Be honest! If you answer yes to any of these 3 questions, eating mindfully is a must! Without conscious awareness your mind goes on auto pilot! Certainly, it's not the best thing for your health or for your waistline!

Although many activities in your body happen on their own, like digestion, heartbeat, or elimination, you need to pay attention to the way you eat if you want to acquire healthy eating habits and maintain your desired weight.

Once upon a time, two young monks were speaking of their Zen masters. The first monk said, "My master is so accomplished he can levitate. In fact, he can even pass-through walls!"

"Well, that's a start," responded the second monk. Astonished, the first monk said, "I'm sure your master cannot do anything more advanced than that!"

The second monk replied, "*Actually, he can. My master is so enlightened that he eats when he is hungry and sleeps when he is tired.*"

This story reminds us of how complicated simple tasks can be, when we have developed years of poor habits, especially eating habits!

Have you ever felt exhausted after a meal, totally drained, unable to concentrate, to center yourself even after a good night's sleep?

Let's look at your blood sugar, which is one factor that should not be overlooked! Don't worry I am not telling you never to touch sweets, all that I am saying is, be aware of how they make you feel. If you experience mood swings and other unwanted symptoms, know that you are out of balance and it's unhealthy for you!

Of course, a small amount of sugar circulating in your blood to fuel your body's metabolic processes is indispensable. Your blood sugar level needs to be steady.

Unfortunately, when you eat too many sweets, your blood sugar will spike and then crash, causing mood swings and other negative symptoms not fun!

As much as you can, choose the "low carb" foods from the low end of the glycemic spectrum, like vegetables, beans, and legumes which curb your appetite, enhance mental alertness, and keep your body energized.

Now, if you are interested in warding off illnesses and strengthening your immune system, I would highly recommend an Alkaline diet.

I have been following it for the last 30 years and I live by it. I rarely get sick, and I have tons of energy! Here's is how it works:

When the blood is too acidic, the body will pull calcium from the bones to neutralize the acid. This causes osteoporosis, and for some, it is the basis for almost all disease.

Nutritional theorist Dr. Robert Young says, "If the acid is left unchecked, it will interrupt all cellular activities and functions from the beating of your heart to the neural-firing of your brain. Over-acidification interferes with life itself…all regulatory systems, including breathing, circulation, digestion, [and] hormone production become exhausted."

To avoid this imbalance, eat alkalizing foods. These include most fruits, vegetables, and seeds. At the same time, reduce your intake of acidic foods such as animal proteins, and all dairy products, like milk and cheese.

The optimum ratio for most people is 75% alkalizing foods to 25% acidifying foods

First thing you must do to maintain an alkaline base for your body is to drink water! Yes, that simple and indispensable! Did you know that mental stress dehydrates your body? And also, you are fatigued and unfocussed? Now remember when you drink water become mindful that this water nourishes the body and keeps you healthy!

In addition to your water intake, I've made a detailed list of those alkalizing food choices for optimum energy and well-being. There are all kinds of vegetables, whole grains, legumes, nuts, and fruits, especi-ally all berries: strawberries, raspberries, blueberries, and apples.

Reduce your intake of wheat and of white flour

Minimize your sugar intake –Watch out for white foods, including refined sugar, potatoes, white flour, and white rice. Beware of sugar lurking in unexpected places! If you decide to indulge in a protein bar, choose a low-carbohydrate one.

- Healthy snacks include almonds, guacamole, edamame, fresh or frozen steamed vegetables.
- Choose olive oil and flax seeds to boost your Omega 3 fatty acids. This is especially important for women's hormonal balance.
- Chew a lot! Remember digestion begins in the mouth.
- Drink herbal teas between meals to flush out your body toxins.

Now, don't think I expect you to be perfect! I'm not perfect either! Remember, I am French and French people enjoy good food, but we tend to pay attention to serving size so we can stay slim and trim. For over 20 years now, I have maintained my ideal weight. The reason I am telling you that, is not to show off, but to show you that you can do it too!

I want to share with you a practice that will help you enjoy food much more and eat much less. It's called the Mindful Eating Practice.

"Five Bite" Technique for Eating

My approach is simple. After 5 bites of any food you eat, put your fork down, sit back, and ask yourself these 3 questions:

1. Do I still taste what I am eating?

2. Am I breathing while I chew? You'll see, this will get you to slow down and enjoy your food much more.
3. Isn't the next bite going to taste the same as the one I just had?

When my clients use this practice, they realize (especially with the last question) that they don't feel like eating more. I am not telling you to have just bites per meal, but to consider 5 bites of the same food and to take the time to assess how you feel.

Just know, it takes much longer for your stomach than your brain to register if you are still hungry or not. So, by stopping to eat after the 5th bite, it gives you a chance to be more in charge of your eating situation.

Now when it comes to dessert, practice the same way, using the 3 questions. Take just 3 bites and enjoy them fully. Keep reminding yourself that the next bite will taste the same as the previous bite and if you finish it all, you will end up with the "sugar blues", bloat, weight gain exhaustion, and lots of guilt. Not a very pretty picture!!!

In order, to help you on this transformational eating journey, I created a delicious and compelling little exercise in mindful eating. You'll need a raisin for this.

This is a completely unforgettable experience which has the power to transform your approach to food forever. I have shared this practice with many clients who suffered from emotional eating issues. When I handed them just one raisin, they invariably laughed, wondering what that tiny piece of fruit could possibly do to help them with their eating! Of course, that's precisely the point.

Ready? Let's give it a try.

Hold that raisin between the thumb and index finger of your favorite hand. Take time to look at it. Notice its smallness, the color of its skin, its texture and shape, the way the light reflects off it.

Slowly and mindfully, bring the raisin to your lips. Bring your full awareness to the experience of its touch and its texture against your lips.

1. Here comes the crucial moment... ever so slowly, place it in your mouth. Feel where this tiny piece of fruit is on your tongue. Note how light it is.
2. Now become aware of your desire to bring your teeth down on it, to bite into it, to eat it. Don't do any of these things just yet. Just be completely aware of these urges by fully observing these reactions.
3. Take some deep breaths and continue to observe yourself without acting or reacting! Sit back in your chair. Relax!
4. Okay, now prepare to act, to do the thing that you so want to do! Place the raisin between your teeth. Hold it there a moment, then slowly, mindfully, bite into it! And continue to maintain absolute awareness of the explosion of flavors that occurs. Surround yourself with the tangy sweetness of the fruit.

VICTIM TO VICTORIOUS

5. Now slowly chew until the raisin fully dissolves, while staying aware of your breathing and how it slows down your chewing.
6. Now the final move: swallow it and focus on the aftertaste lingering on your tongue.

Voila! Victory to you!

For most people, this experience leads to the realization that when they eat normally, they rarely take the time to savor, to fully taste their food. Imagine, for a moment, always eating this way. Imagine eating slowly, mindfully, enjoying the multi-layered sensations of food textures, colors, smells and flavors...

Can you see the positive implications of such a mindful eating practice? Eating mindfully completely magnifies the pleasures of food, leading you to eat less and enjoy more. I also understand it's not that easy to adopt and enjoy this new lifestyle. But I promise you that, through repetition you will create this new habit and behavior. 28 days of practice is the time I recommend, to achieve this result. For now, just remember that you can slow down, enjoy your food more and in doing so, you'll enjoy the benefits of eating less while giving nothing up in return. Just the opposite!

In fact, recall this experience in the days and meals to follow. Change begins in awareness! In dreams, responsibilities begin ...

Used together, the Five Bite technique and Mindful Eating can transform both your eating experience and your waistline--an unbeatable combination! Work at it, practice! Give yourself time and make it your goal to become a mindful eater and to appreciate the enormous benefits of such a behavior. Victory to you!

VICTIM TO VICTORIOUS

Meditation to Inspire You on the Journey

"The Lighthouse"

TO RESTORE HEALTH

Sit comfortably and breathe deeply

Think of a place in your body that brings you discomfort— such as a muscle, an organ, anything you experience. Bring your awareness to this area now. Accept the pain without any judgment yourself— Ask yourself: is it sharp, dull, throbbing or piercing? Hot or cold? Study it without reacting to it.

Now move your awareness to your heart and imagine a luminous  *diamond at its very center. As you keep picturing it, it becomes clearer, radiating pure light.*

See yourself as a lighthouse sending out a powerful, sweeping beam of light into the darkness and through your own body. Imagine now this beam dissolving the pain and revitalizing the surrounding tissues. Send the light everywhere in your body. You are the keeper of the lighthouse, keeping it safe, vibrant, and healthy.

THINK TO YOURSELF:

My body is created by infinite intelligence.

VICTIM TO VICTORIOUS

My subconscious mind knows how to heal me.
It is now transforming every cell of my body, making me healthy and whole.

Chapter 5

Dexxtra

Congratulations! Now we have finished exploring the many facets of the Mindfulness experience, from a Meditation walk to mindful eating! You're now ready for DEXXTRA, the last practice to complete Step 1 Clear.

Before we discuss everything, you need to know about DEXXTRA, I want to talk about Emotions! Think of the word Emotion, the letter E could stand for energy, don't you think? so we end up with Energy in motion. When you feel angry for instance, you experience lots of energy. You move fast, you usually talk louder and faster, your heart rate goes up, your blood pressure rises, you turn red in the face... there's a lot going on in the body! The opposite happens when you feel sad. The body activities slow down, you barely move, your breathing is shallow and slow, you don't say much, there's very little going on! These emotions and reactions are part of our lives! We cannot live without them, although sometimes we refuse to deal with them and repress them...

We push them down and try to convince ourselves that we shouldn't feel this way! To do so is foolish and unreasonable! Accept the emotions and accept that being emotional means being human…it's a normal thing! Stop labeling emotions as either negative or positive, good, or bad. What really matters is whether they **support** you and make you feel good, or they **sabotage** you and rob you of pleasure and joy in your life.

To give you an example: being afraid of speaking in front of people is totally understandable and normal, but to refuse to show up and to do your best because of your fear is not! That's why I created Dexxtra to show you how to make those emotions **work for you.**

Dexxtra stands for **Extra Stress Release** at your fingertips. It offers an innovative "anywhere anytime" acupressure-based technique which works wonders with stress. It alleviates and balances blocked feelings and frustrated emotions. As you know, stress creates toxicity in the body. Dexxtra activates the body's own ability to restore vitality and strength. It came into being as the result of years of my studies of both Eastern and Western practices. It's my favorite technique, the one I use the most, and I think you will too!

So, this is how Dexxtra works: There are 5 major emotions you are going to work with, which are: Worry, fear, anger sadness and overwhelm.

You have 5 fingers (counting the thumb), with each one representing a particular emotion. To help you remember, here's a shortcut to represent each one of the 5 emotions: "**Worry Fast**". The thumb is "**W**" for worry, the index finger is "**F**" for fear, the middle finger is, as one might expect, "**A**" for anger, the ring finger is "**S**" for sadness, and the little finger is "**T**" for trying hard or overwhelmed. In addition to holding the finger, you have special sounds that go with each one. It's a serious exercise but also fun and easy to use, you'll see why in a minute!

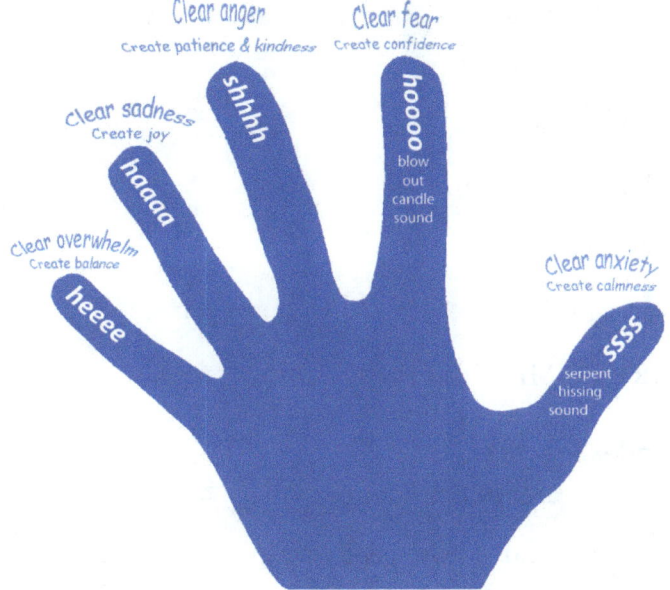

1. The Thumb Practice:
To Clear Anxiety, Create Calmness

Let's start by breathing deeply and slowly. Gently wrap your left thumb with the fingers of your right hand. As you hold, take a deep breath in and on the exhalation make a" Serpent **hissing**" sound **SSS**. Repeat 2 more times. Then focus your attention on your thumb, feeling a pulsing sensation going on. Now imagine all of your worries have melted away. Smile at this **Calming** experience! Accepting it with appreciation and gratitude and then you declare out loud or to yourself:

I choose to be Calm

I am willing to be Calm

I desire to be Calm

I believe that I Can

VICTORY TO ME!

2. The Index Practice:
To Clear Fear, Create Confidence

Breathe deeply and slowly, gently wrap your left index finger with the fingers of your right hand. As you hold, take a deep breath in and on the exhalation make a "**blowing out candle**" sound **HOOOO**. Repeat 2 more times, then focus your attention on your index, feeling a pulsing sensation going on. Imagine all your fears have melted away. Smile at this **Confidence** experience! Accept it with appreciation and gratitude and then you declare out loud or to yourself:

I choose to be Confident

I am willing to be Confident

I desire to be Confident

I believe that I Can

VICTORY TO ME!

3. The Middle Finger Practice:
Clear Anger, Create Patience

Breathe deeply and slowly, gently wrap your middle finger with the fingers of your right hand. As you hold, take a deep breath in and on the exhalation make a sound **SHHHH. Repeat** 2 more times, then focus your attention on your middle, feeling a pulsing sensation going on. Imagine all your anger has melted away. Smile at this **Patience and Kindness** experience! accept it with appreciation and gratitude and then you declare out loud or to yourself:

I choose to be Patient and Kind

I am willing to be Patient and Kind

I desire to be Patient and Kind

I believe that I Can

VICTORY TO ME!

4. The Ring Finger Practice:
Clear Sadness, Create Joy

Breathe deeply and slowly, gently wrap your ring finger with the fingers of your right hand. As you hold, take a deep breath in and on the exhalation make a sound **HAAAA. Repeat** 2 more times, then focus your attention on your ring finger, feeling a pulsing sensation going on. Imagine all your sadness has melted away. Smile at this

Joyful experience! Accept it with appreciation and gratitude and then you declare out loud or to yourself:

I choose to be Joyful

I am willing to be Joyful

I desire to be Joyful

I believe that I Can

VICTORY TO ME!

**5. The Little Finger Practice:
Clear Overwhelm, Create Balance**

Breathe deeply and slowly, gently wrap your little finger with the fingers of your right hand. As you hold, take a deep breath in and on the exhalation make a sound **HEEEE. Repeat** 2 more times, then focus your attention on your little finger, feeling a pulsing sensation going on. Imagine all the overwhelm has melted away. Smile at this **Balance** experience! Accept it with appreciation and gratitude and then you declare out loud or to yourself:

I choose to be balanced and centered

I am willing to be balanced and centered

I desire to be balanced and centered

I believe that I Can

VICTORY TO ME!

Victory to you, Victory is yours! You've made it to DEXXTRA!

I understand that I've given you lots of information and techniques! It feels like there's a lot to memorize, but it's ok! Please relax, take a deep breath, and know that you don't have to do it all! Just choose what you need the most and what works best for you. With DEXXTRA, you could start with just 2 fingers for instance!

My clients and I all enjoy the Worry Thumb and Fear Index finger the most, because we all encounter challenging situations that require us to stay calm and confident to deal with them successfully. As far as the Mindfulness Meditation goes, I insist that you practice the 3C's every day, because if you recall, it's the foundation for feeling safe within. We all know that today more than ever, we cannot rely on the outside world to do that job for us.

So, at this point, choose a time, (starting today) to do your 3C's, commit to it, because as you already know, it's the only way it works!

Chapter 6

Create

CREATE! Such a hopeful word filled with mystery, potential and possibilities. This is exactly what I intend to offer you now!

Get ready to discover a new life transforming language, and to delve into the awesome power of your imagination.

The Cherokee Parable of the Two Wolves

One evening an old Cherokee told his grandson about an ancient battle. A never-ending conflict that goes on still. He said, "My son, there is a battle, a war between two wolves that inhabit us all. One wolf loves to feed on anger, envy, jealousy, sadness, regret, greed, arrogance and

self-pity... the other one loves to feed on joy, peace, love, hope, serenity, humility, kindness, benevolence and compassion."

The grandson considered the elder's words for a moment. It seemed true, what the grandfather said, yet he was troubled by one question. Raising his eyes to meet the old man's he asked: "Grandfather, which wolf wins?" The old Cherokee smiled at the question and then replied simply, "The one you feed the most."

Most of us are so critical of ourselves! We are our own worst enemies! We think we are not good enough... we should be better looking, more accomplished, more intelligent, more this, more that.... We carry shame, guilt, and a poor self-image from childhood into our adult lives. We employ it in constant judgment of our failures and shortcomings. In other words, we feed the wrong wolf! It grows stronger and stronger every day, while the other one grows weaker and weaker every day. We must change this!

Why do we feed the wrong wolf - the Inner Critic? Why do we accept criticism and judgment from ourselves when we resent receiving it from others? The reason is devastatingly simple: For most of us, it's the only language we know! It's stored in the old recordings of the *"subconscious library"*. It's the language we learn as children, the only language we understand, but if we want to be happy, it's time to get rid of it!

Of course, it's going to take some time and practice, but it can be done! First, you need to become aware of the old voice, to hear it distinctly, to recognize it for what it is, a toxic and useless tongue! Once you have done that, you understand you have a choice in the words you use. There is another language out there, sweet, quite beautiful to the ear! It is called the language of the heart.

VICTIM TO VICTORIOUS

VICTIM TO VICTORIOUS

Meditation to Inspire You on the Journey

"The sword of light"

TO DEVELOP STRENGTH AND FEARLESSNESS

Sit comfortably and breathe deeply.

Imagine you are in some outdoor space, perhaps a forest. You are standing, legs, trunk and feet firmly rooted to the earth. It's a warm and sunny day and there is an invigorating wind blowing in the air. Your body is alert but relaxed, your mind is free.

Conjure up a specific goal you want to accomplish. Perhaps it's making a phone call you've been putting off or expressing your feelings to a loved one? Anything challenging that needs your attention!

Now picture yourself approaching the actual scene with a sword of light in your hand. Look at your sword. Its blade shines in the sun and as you move forward with it in your hand, it reflects brilliant rays of powerful light. Have fun with this. Perhaps you are King Arthur, Conan the Barbarian or Xeena the warrior princess.

Feel how purposeful you are now that you hold the power of the sword of light in your hand. Think again about your goal. Take the energy of the sun with the sword and transform it into the energy of absolute power and conviction. Know you can move forward to the destiny of this event with great courage and confidence. All fear and doubt have been banished.

DECLARE TO YOURSELF:

My breath is calm and effortless.
I breathe into my belly, my power center.
I feel my strength, my courage.
I feel unstoppable.
I am ready to act.
I can, I do, I will.

Part I The Language of the Heart

It all begins with love! When you treat your**self** as a friend, as a loved one, you begin to cultivate emotional balance and experience more joy!

Do you think you can learn to speak to yourself with support and understanding? Please remember that the most important words you will ever hear are the ones you tell yourself every day! I know it's kind of strange at first! Just start stop "**shoulding** on yourself" and saying *I can't* too many times! Instead, begin to favor "I choose, I can, I give myself permission, I am willing!" Notice how you feel when you do!

Now, as you begin to practice the language of the heart, prepare to encounter resistance. Why? Because the old language is familiar to you! It's all you have known for so many years! So be patient and loving with yourself! And here is a technique which you can use when you catch yourself being self-critical: simply recognize that foreign and toxic tongue! And realize that you are feeding this unhappy wolf, who savors that food you are giving him! Then, without any judgment whatsoever, say to yourself the word CANCEL!

It interrupts the old pattern, creating a blank mental screen, where you can write loving words and feed the **other** wolf! Practice makes perfect and in time, this new language of the heart gets recorded in the *"subconscious library"* and begins to get airplay. As you play it back, you get to appreciate its cadences and harmonies!

It becomes sweetness to your ears, and you begin to tune into it more! In response to its popularity, new recordings are being stored and played back. Soon the number of the language of the heart recordings will equal and outnumber the old hits! So, begin to record! Begin to practice the language of the heart and turn your *inner Critic* into your *inner Coach!*

Victory to You! You are amazing! pat yourself on the back and say to yourself" I am amazing! Victory to ME! Victory is MINE!

I know it may sound a little strange at first but give it a try! What have you got to lose? Discover the joy of counting your victories at the end of the day, instead of most people counting their defeats. To also help you on this transformational journey, I have made a list of words which have changed my life and the lives of thousands of my clients. And by the way, I still use these words today, and I intend to use them for the rest of my life, because I love the way they make me feel!

Remember the sequence:

VICTIM TO VICTORIOUS

Thoughts --- Feelings --- Actions --- Results

Remember if you are not aware of the **thought** that gets you to feel the way you do, just get in touch with the **feeling** and figure out how you can make it work **for you** and turn it into strength. Go into your toolbox and decide what can help you at this moment. Maybe it's Dexxtra? Maybe the 3C's? Or perhaps a nice mindful walk? You see, you always have the option to do something that can put you back on course and can also boost your mental clarity and self-confidence!

Vocabulary for the Language of the Heart

Are you ready and willing to ban the words of the Critic?

"I should" ... Stop "shoulding on yourself"! It does not work!

"I cannot" ... Stop shutting yourself down! It is not worth it!

"I have to" ... Stop putting pressure on yourself! It is useless!

Are you ready and willing to practice the words of the inner Coach?

"I choose" ... You feel in control, and you have choices!

"I can" ... You have infinite possibilities to try new things!

"I desire." ... You get to move towards your selected goal!

Are you beginning to understand the difference it makes in your emotional energy when you shift from the language of the **hurt** to the language of the **heart**?

When I experienced this shift, I was able to end my binge eating disorder and resumed my modelling career. I felt reborn! I stopped being a "poor thing", a sad victimized me! I became invincible, unstoppable. I was finally in charge of my destiny! Free to be who I was born to be! No one and nothing could stop me anymore and the most amazing part was that it was so simple! Just by choosing different words I could transform myself from the inside out and you can too!

Just know that for the language of the heart, you have the freedom to invent the vocabulary you want!

Keep in mind these 3 important things when you do:

- Consider positive assertive statements that say YES to your potential. They are called your affirmations- your claim to a powerful life.
- For the affirmations to work faster, repeat them over and over with enthusiasm and confidence, so that they become empowering beliefs and create success!
- Your chosen affirmations need to have 3 P's:

1. **Personal** Use the first person singular "I"
2. **Positive** State what you **want** and not **what you don't** want anymore
3. **Present** Use the present tense only. The subconscious mind only relates to the **now.**

I love the 3 P's! they're easy to remember and to use! For years now, every morning my daily 3 P's have been the following:

"I am happy to be me, I welcome the day filled with infinite possibilities, I Can, I Do, I will! Victory to me! Victory is mine" It really works wonders and prepares me for a great day! If you like this one, feel free to use it!

FOOD FOR THOUGHT

"You become what you think you are."

-BUDDHA

"You are the total sum of your thoughts!"

-BUDDHA

"Whatever words we utter should be chosen with care, for people will hear them and be influenced by them for good or ill."

-BUDDHA

Change can happen at the speed of thought, and in your heart, you know it's not a joke! Your thoughts become your destiny! And you also know deep down that you truly **deserve** to be happy. It's time for you to turn the page and to claim your victory!

Share the language of the heart with your loved ones, your friends, and the whole world!!! After all, it needs it badly, don't you think?

VICTORY TO YOU and VICTORY to all of us!

VICTIM TO VICTORIOUS

Meditation to Inspire You on the Journey

"Armor of the Light"

FOR PROTECTION

Sit comfortably and breathe deeply

This meditation is inspired by the 7 Chakras of the Yoga tradition. In this practice the focus is on just 3 of them to bring a state of mind/body balance.

Imagine you are surrounded by a circle of divine sparkling white light that protects you like a warrior's shield. The light penetrates each cell of your body – your blood cells, your muscles, your organs, your bones, your skin. The light brings you a sense of absolute well-being. You are bathed in that divine light which restores your balance and prevents negative energy from reaching you. Only godly things can enter your life now. You are protected.

Put a little smile on your face to appreciate this experience. Send that smiling energy down to your belly. It's your third Chakra, it's the center of courage, strength, and will. To activate this power center, imagine your belly covered with the bright yellow light of the sun.

*Affirm to yourself: **"I can…I create…I manifest."***

Next, bring your smiling energy up to your fourth Chakra, the heart, center of compassion, and kindness. To activate this center, imagine your chest covered with the bright green light of the meadows. Affirm to yourself: **"I embrace life with honesty and love".**

Finally, bring your smiling energy up to the middle of your forehead, the six Chakra, center of wisdom, guidance, and intuition. To activate it, imagine your forehead covered with the purple light of the amethyst stone.

Affirm to yourself: **"I trust that I will be guided towards my highest good and purpose."**

Now that you have activated each one of the 3 centers with your attention and smiling energy, take a moment to bask in the light that protects you.

THINK TO YOURSELF:

*"I feel the light surrounding me now.
It serves as a shield of protection.
Only good and loving things are coming into my life. With intention and conviction, I reject all negativity."*

Part II Mindful Questions

Before completing the chapter on the Language of the Heart, I wish to add one last thing that makes a big difference, which is the power of mindful questions. Those are the questions you ponder in the dark and in the privacy of your own mind, that influence your behavior and your decision making.

VICTIM TO VICTORIOUS

Why do we call them restrooms when no one goes there to rest?

Why do you give your two cents worth when it's only a penny for your thoughts?

No, these are not the questions I am talking about, but I chose them to provoke some laughter! We all need a little!

The serious questions I want to address are those mindful ones, which can change the course of your life, and which happen at the speed of thought.

Mindful Questions

One golden rule on this matter: promise yourself that no matter what the situation is, never ask why it happens, but instead what am I learning from this!

Just know that if you ask why me? The automatic answer is going to be - because I am an idiot, or I am unlucky and the worst one of them all is because I am a loser. On the other hand, when you begin to ask what I am learning, you'll hear the lessons you need to learn to grow in spirit and have a better quality of life!

Here is the list of 7 mindful questions I have selected for you! I expect you to take them seriously and of course answer them!

1. How do I feel right now?

Whatever the answer is: angry fearful or unhappy, make sure you don't turn them into affirmations like I am angry, I am afraid, or I am sad, because not matter what you feel, realize that it's not a permanent condition, so it's best to say I feel angry, I feel afraid, I feel sad. Keep the "I am" statements for your desired states, such as I am calm, I am confident, or I am happy. Notice the difference it makes when you do! And if seriously stressed, use the **Dexxtra practice!**

2. What is your intention?

Before you take any action or make any decision, always ask yourself that question, then picture your desired outcome while feeling good about it.

3. What is a habit/behavior you wish to change?

Be specific in your thinking process and choose the most important one that is seriously affecting the quality of your life. For example: overeating, excess drinking, lack of physical exercise.

4. What do I want instead?

Choose a healthy habit/behavior to replace the unwanted one. For instance, instead of coming home and reaching for a glass of wine, prepare a hot tea. Warm temperature is soothing to the body and calming to the mind.

5. What stops me from changing this habit?

Examine your emotions. Are you feeling an emptiness inside and using your habit to fill up that space?

6. How will my life change when i develop this new habit or behavior?

You could consider improving your health, losing weight, getting into shape, gaining more peace of mind and experiencing enthusiasm for your life.

VICTIM TO VICTORIOUS

7. What action can I take right now to create this desired change?

Whatever action you choose to take, make sure you schedule it and get accountability for it. For instance, going to the gym, preparing healthy meals.

Keep these questions fresh in your mind because the *Screening Room Practice* is coming up soon!

Meditation to Inspire You on the Journey

"The Horizon"

TO DEVELOP INNER STRENGTH

Sit comfortably and breathe deeply

Imagine you are steadily climbing a rock face. The climb requires some strategy and effort, but you can handle it. You are strong and agile and filled with enthusiasm and vibrant energy. You look down, you see pine trees, you look up, you notice the top of the cliff, and above a clear blue sky. Your breathing feels deep and steady. You have strength in your arms and legs, and your fingers are connecting to the rocks. You clip your harness a little tighter and keep moving. You feel the power of your leg muscles pushing you up the rock face. The summit is approaching, and with a final push, you are up and over the edge.

You stand on the mountaintop, the world at your feet. The air is crystal clear. You can see farther and wider than you ever imagined. You look out at the horizon and see your bright future!

DECLARE TO YOURSELF:

"I choose to have the best future I can imagine. To make this future real, I pursue it with all my heart, I do the best I can with what I know, and I keep my focus on the outcome."

Part III The Screening Room Practice

There is a story about a young man who went in search of a particular enlightened master. He went from town to town until someone pointed out an old man.

The seeker asked the Master, "What did you do before your Enlightenment?" The Master replied, "Chopped wood and carried water from the well."

"And now that you have become enlightened, what do you do now?"

The Master responded, "Chop wood and carry water."

The Seeker was troubled by this. Puzzled, he asked, "But what has changed then?"

VICTIM TO VICTORIOUS

The Master answered, "The difference is on the inside. Before I was doing everything in my sleep, now I am awake. The world is still the same, yet I have changed; therefore, the world is different for me. "

With the Screening Room Practice you awaken; you experience the beginnings of a master's enlightenment. I know you are already feeling different doing the same things: Practicing your 3C's, eating and walking mindfully. You begin to trust in your ability to turn your stress into strength, shift from victim to victory gaining more emotional balance and energy.

Such behavior changes are going to be evident in *"The Screening Room"*. With each daily visit, the projected pictures and feelings of visualized desired change will become more vivid and more real to you. In time, they will become you... You see, the mind cannot distinguish between what's real and what's vividly imagined, so what you imagine can make as powerful of an impression on your subconscious mind, as real events can.

The Screening Room helps you develop positive expectations. This is important because your expectations will be fulfilled. Watch what you wish for! It's called the "law of attraction". Esther-hicks and the teachings of Abraham teaches this concept that your thoughts attract your reality. If disaster is all you can imagine, then disaster is what you create! On the other hand, if you visualize what you desire, believe, and imagine, you can and will create!

Take me for example; when I first moved to NYC, I did not believe I could have my dream apartment. So, I ended up in the smallest darkest, murphy bed, cold studio. Once I learned about the law of attraction, I decided to apply it. Every day for 28 days I walked my dog past this ideal building, I would look up and pictured myself living on the top floor with a beautiful view. A month later I made it happen and I claimed my Victory!

This practice is based on self-hypnosis and for it to work, you need daily repetitions. Let me tell you why: Think of planting a new seed, which is a metaphor for your desired change. You do know that for this seed to grow and flourish, you need to water it every day.

This is how the Screening room practice works! You begin to feel your change and see your growth within 28 days.

The first step to prepare for this practice is to decide what you seriously need to create in your life. List all the specific indications of that change. Now take this process to the next level. What other positive outcomes can be generated by your change? What are the larger repercussions? Now that you have energy, momentum, courage, and optimism, what else can you do? If you choose to lose 10 pounds for example, begin to picture yourself reaching this goal, see yourself gaining momentum, notice your energy spiraling upward, feeling good about yourself and having more self-esteem.

Believe you can achieve this goal, that nothing can stop you from even greater life change. Experience doing more with greater ease... day after day. Begin to dare to reach for other greater goals. You are on a roll! You are passionate and unstoppable! Make sure you see and feel both the impact of reaching this goal as well as its effect on your health, your relationships, your career, and your social life. In addition, I strongly recommend that you record this practice (you can use your phone or for additional customized help, contact me), so that you can relax and get its full benefits. It's best to practice in the morning to prepare for a productive and joyful day.

VICTIM TO VICTORIOUS

The Screening Room Practice

How to Create the Future You Desire

1. Look up at the ceiling. Take 3 or 4 deep breaths to relax. Inhale through the nose and exhale through the mouth,

> SAY TO YOURSELF,
> PREFERABLY ALOUD:
>
> *"As I watch this spot on the ceiling, my eyelids are becoming heavier and heavier. So heavy, that my eyes want to close, and I feel completely and totally relaxed now*

2. Repeat this phrase a few times, until you feel your eyes wanting to close.

> AS YOUR EYES CLOSE,
> SAY TO YOURSELF:
>
> *Relax now... let go... deeper now.*
> *Relax now... let go... deeper now.*

3. Begin to explore the sensations of your body. Feel your shoulders letting go of tensions, your arms feeling heavy, your legs feeling loose and limp. Notice your body becoming totally relaxed.

4. You are now ready to go deeper into a state of hypnosis.

> SAY TO YOURSELF OUT LOUD:
>
> *"Now I am going deeper and deeper...*
> *Now I am going deeper and deeper...*
> *deeper and deeper now..."*

Continue to repeat this phrase until you experience what you are telling yourself.

5. Then imagine yourself standing at the top of a staircase going down 5 steps. As you descend the steps, count backwards from 5 to 1. With each number you hear and each step you take, you are reaching a very peaceful and safe place.

6. Once you reach the bottom of the staircase, you find yourself in a hallway. Walk down the hallway at your own pace feeling safe and notice a door with an inscription that reads "Screening Room." Push the door open and enter the room. In the center, you see a comfortable chair facing a big movie screen. Go and sit in this chair. The moment you do you become the scriptwriter director and star of your show. Project in detail the scene that illustrates your desired goal. See yourself doing what you want to do, looking the way you want to look, and feeling good about yourself.

Allow yourself to fully experience the feeling of success and joy.

> AS YOU WATCH THIS MOVIE
> PROJECTED ON THE SCREEN,
> SAY TO YOURSELF OUT LOUD:
>
> *I choose to have this experience.*
> *I can have this experience.*
> *I am now creating this experience every day in every way.*

7. Place a smile on your face, to savor this moment and to anchor this peak positive experience at the cellular level of your body. Then make a fist with your non-dominant hand and repeat 3 times aloud: "**Victory to me. Victory is mine.**" Know that these words are precious and are the indispensable password to access your transformation. During the day repeat these words as often as possible, while making a fist with your non-dominant hand. Each time you do, you activate the memory of this experience.

8. It's time to come back feeling refreshed, excited, and expecting to have your desired results. Walk back down the hallway to the

stairway. Walk up the steps, counting from 1 to 5. When you reach number 5, open your eyes and smile with gratitude and appreciation for this new experience.

How did you do? Remember, this is your first time! Although you may not have reached the deepest state of Alpha where change takes place, today you have taken an important step in this essential practice. I promise that each time you do, you become more and more skillful in your use of the Screening Room. Practice makes it perfect right? or at least close enough!!!

Be patient, re-read the Hypnosis script, listen to the recording, if possible, memorize the script, and practice. Feel free to add more details to your home movie. Go easy with yourself if you forget some of the words. The key words which you will want to remember are Relax... Let Go... Deeper Now and your password *Victory to me, Victory is mine.*

Meditation to Inspire You on the Journey

"The Garden of the Heart"

TO CONNECT TO YOURSELF WITH LOVE

VICTIM TO VICTORIOUS

Sit comfortably and breathe deeply.

Imagine you are sitting comfortably looking at a bouquet of flowers. Begin to focus all your attention on your favorite flower. Stare at it, breathe in its scent, feel its beauty, and imagine that this flower belongs to your heart, to the garden of your heart. In this garden, everything is perfect and magnificent. See what you see and  *when you feel ready, take the flower in your hands, and place it over your heart. As you hold the flower, focus your attention on your breath, breathe into your heart and plant the flower in its center. Nurture it with a loving smile. Know that from now on, you are the gardener of your heart, and you make your garden grow. Take pride in cultivating it and be the witness to the beauty of your blossoming joy.*

Chapter 7

Next Step

Experts say you can relieve your stress by petting a cat. Of course, it doesn't work if the cat is the one making you nuts in the first place! Don't worry about feeling stressed, some rocks become diamonds under extreme pressure, and for the other rocks, they just turn into dust no big deal!

I hope I gave you a good laugh which as we know, is good for your stress! I also know that releasing stress is not as easy as it sounds, especially if you only have read the "***Fresh Start Program***" once! So, to make sure you get what you want from my program, I want to lay out a step-by-step plan to show you how to incorporate the **Clear and Create** techniques in your everyday life.

Your 28 Day Fresh Start Program

It is divided into 4 parts, morning, afternoon, evening, and bedtime.

1. **Morning practice (10 minutes)**
   - Square breathing practice to focus your mind

- 3C's Mindfulness meditation practice to become Calm, Centered and Connected throughout your day
- The Mindful question "What is my intention today?" In other words what do I want to accomplish which will make me feel good about myself?
- To seal this morning practice, add the Metta prayer which is a Buddhist tradition for loving kindness. I love this because first it starts by calling in the blessings to oneself, then it's sent to a loved one (best to visualize the person you send it to) and ends with sending the loving kindness to everyone, which we all need;

May I be safe and protected
May I be healthy and strong
May I be peaceful, loving, and joyful

May you be safe and protected
May you be healthy and strong
May you be peaceful, loving, and joyful

May we be safe and protected
May we be healthy and strong
May we be peaceful, loving, and joyful

PS: Have a Mindful breakfast

2. **Afternoon practice (10 minutes)**
   - *Mindful question "How do I feel right now?"* to help you get in touch with your feelings! If the answer is not to your satisfaction, practice *Dexxtra* Identify one of the 5 unwanted

emotions: anxiety, insecurity, anger, sadness, and a sense of being overwhelmed.
- Use the *Language of the Heart* (page 52)? And declare out loud or to yourself:

"I Can, I Do, I Will! Victory to me, Victory is mine."

Repeat this affirmation 2 to 3 times to yourself or out loud to deepen the new connection and to maintain good energy throughout the day.

PS: Take a mindful walk

3. Evening practice (10 minutes)

- *Count your victories.* Preferably write down the things that you have done well today. For example, "I chose a healthy salad for lunch instead of a hamburger" or "Although I felt tired, I went for a walk". Hope you get the idea! It does not have to be big, but just notice little changes occurring every day and in every way!
- *Activate your password from the Screening Room: Victory to me, Victory is mine.*

PS: Have a mindful dinner

4. Night time practice (15 minutes)

Practice lying down in bed, ideal and most beneficial time to practice both the **Clear and Create** techniques

- Square breathing practice

- the 3C's Mindfulness Meditation to clear your agitation from the day and finish up with
- the Screening room to create the desired vision for your new life!

PS: Have nice dreams

Keep in mind that this 45-minute investment every day, will improve the other 23 hours and 15 minutes of the rest of your day and within 28 days your life will be changed forever! Irresistible offer, right?

Practice every day!

YOU CAN DO THIS! VICTORY IS YOURS!

Chapter 8

Looking Forward

So now that you have your 28-day plan, you may wonder what other plan you need to follow for the rest of your life?

FOOD FOR THOUGHT

"Happiness is when what you think, what you say and what you do are in harmony."

-MOHANDAS GANDHI

"Life is an empty canvas; it becomes whatsoever you paint on it. You can paint misery, you can paint bliss, this freedom is your glory."

-OSHO

VICTIM TO VICTORIOUS

"Who looks outside, dreams, who looks inside, awakens."

-CARL JUNG

"Happiness is not achieved by the conscious pursuit of happiness; it is generally the by-product of other activities."

-ALDOUS HUXLEY

There once was a man desperate for the meaning of life. He had taken all known routes along the path. Not only had he filled his library with new age books, but also his garage. He had become a yoga adept and could bend his body in 12 different directions. Despite all that, he still did not have the answer he wanted, and hoped that some wise and saintly soul existed somewhere in the universe who would give it to him.

One day, he heard about this old wise monk who lived in a mountain cave high in the obscure region of the Himalayas. He enlisted a Sherpa guide and began the long, arduous trek to his destination. On the final day of the journey he suffered sub-zero temperatures, endured oxygen depletion, and nearly died in a terrible blizzard. He was led to the master who sat serenely in the mouth of the mountain cave. Prostrating himself before the wisest of the wise, the man finally asked the question that had so consumed him. "Please, Master, tell me, what is the meaning of this life?" The old master sighed, took a deep breath and replied, "Life is a fountain". Unable to quite believe his ears, the man became perplexed and said "Please, Master, I am in no condition for such jokes. I beg of you, to answer seriously the question that has nearly destroyed my life." A puzzled look filled the Master's face "So let me get this straight," he said, "life isn't like a fountain?"

Welcome to the rest of your life! Now is a time to discover why you are here and what your life purpose is!

I hope you will forgive me, but there are no techniques or definite answers on this topic! What I can do is share my experiences with you, which can guide you.

In my twenties, I was stranded on a deserted Bahamian island at a serious Yoga ashram. I was studying for an entire month at this secluded center, hoping to gain my certification as an instructor. The regiment was Spartan: in bed by 8:30 pm, up before sunrise to do Sanskrit chanting, followed by arduous physical exertions throughout the entire day. After a week, I was, quite frankly, a resentful young French woman. Gone was the make-up, the jewelry, the sexy dresses. Instead, I was forced to wear a coarse saffron tunic, instructed to be buttoned up to the neck, with a pair of white cotton baggy pants, which were the plainest piece of clothing I had ever worn. Had I given up my French identity, my "joie de vivre"? For what? Military life? If this was the path towards enlightenment, maybe it wasn't for me!

Sometime during the second week, unable to sleep, I heard what seemed like distant drumming. Without giving it a second thought, I jumped out of bed, put a sexy dress on, walked out of my room and started to run on the beach, towards the sound of this irresistible music.

The moon was full, and its light danced across the sea. Sooner than I had imagined, I was within sight of the island's other compound. Now, along with the pulsing rhythm of the music, I could hear other sounds, a cacophony of human voices. "Are you from the yoga place?" A voice finally spoke. "Yes," I nodded. The door swung open, "Welcome to Club Med," he said.

I could have danced all night, and that night I surely did! After the austerity of the yoga boot camp, my new discovery was truly heaven sent. I felt exuberant, alive. Every day after that, I woke up at 5:00 am, enjoyed the chanting, the yoga postures, even the ancient texts.

Every night I jumped the fence, put grooves on the dance floor and mixed music with meditation. I found my way to feed my body and fill my soul with joy!

"Without judgment, everything is perfect".

Follow your passion, follow your inspiration and do it your way. Become aware that passion is energy! Yes, it is that simple! It's energy that you feel when you do what you love, that which makes you happy! And the good news is that the answer is inside you! For me it's music, dance and guiding people on their life path and purpose! Ask yourself, *"What makes me happy?"* and don't judge the answer!

Begin to realize that your answer is not to be found outside of yourself, in *the object*, in the material in possession of *the thing*. Pay attention to how you are being lured into possessing the *thing*. It is hard to resist! Whether it is the latest cell phone, the laptop, the designer sneakers, or handbag, we all crave that *thing*! When you finally get that *thing*, the joy is short lived. The feeling of possession is never quite as good as we'd imagined! Sometimes we can be disappointed, depressed, even angry, that the *things* don't bring the happiness we thought they would! They also become outdated, and we end up with old *things* and we feel like a poor *thing*! And on it goes!

FOOD FOR THOUGHT

"Compassion is the ultimate and most meaningful embodiment of emotional maturity. It is through compassion that a person achieves the highest peak and deepest reach in his or her search for self-fulfillment. "

-ARTHUR JERSILD

"Never apologize for showing feelings, when you do so, you apologize for the truth"

-BENJAMIN DISRAELI

"I would rather feel compassion than know the meaning of it"

-THOMAS AQUINAS

"If you want others to be happy, practice compassion.

VICTIM TO VICTORIOUS

> *If you want to be happy, practice compassion."*
>
> -THE DALI LAMA

Chapter 9

Signposts For Your Spiritual Journey

I hope you realize by now that **you** and **only** you are in possession of the plan for the rest of your life and that it includes finding the meaning of your life and realizing that the answer resides in the spirit deep inside you! So, to assist you on this new quest, I have made a list of signposts that will indicate you are on the right track and that you are becoming a serious spiritual being!

- You become aware of your defense mechanisms and those mechanisms begin to fall away.
- You become more and more clear to yourself and others every day.
- You are more present, able to immerse yourself in the moment!
- You become more creative and imaginative.
- You feel the gentle voice of intuition leading you on the path, and you trust that voice.

- You stop taking things so seriously and learn to find the fun.
- You believe that every day is filled with infinite possibilities.
- You stop focusing on what the ego wants and you start focusing on your highest good.
- You have the courage to look at yourself and the willingness to transform your beliefs to create positive outcomes.
- You stop blaming others and taking responsibility for yourself.
- You know that if you happen to be "made to feel" badly around others, it's an illusion, something the ego creates.
- You realize that people have no power over you, it's only your reaction that gives them power and you can change that.
- You realize that *difficult* people, are *different*. Their actions are the result of their childhood and the conditions that shaped them.
- You realize that difficult people are your greatest teachers, teaching patience tolerance and unconditional love.
- You stop wanting to change those people and you start treating them with compassion.
- You believe that if we treat people the way we would like them to be they might become that way.
- You attract like-minded people, who are invested in love honesty and integrity.

VICTIM TO VICTORIOUS

Meditation to Inspire You on the Journey

"The Satellite"

TO RECONCILE YOURSELF TO OTHERS.

Sit comfortably and breathe deeply.

Imagine that you are a satellite which is both a receiver and transmitter of energy. This energy travels around the globe. You always broadcast, whether you are aware of it or not. Imagine that you broadcast loving kindness throughout the world. Start by sending a transmission to the ones you love dearly. Visualize their faces. Now broadcast the same loving kindness to an acquaintance, one you know, but do not necessarily love. Again, concentrate on this person's face. Finally, think of one person who has hurt or wronged you. Take time to do this, it's not easy! This person has also suffered and might still be suffering. Send this person compassion and loving kindness and imagine the possibility of harmony between the two of you now.

VICTIM TO VICTORIOUS

> **THINK TO YOURSELF**
>
> *I recognize that each person is different.*
> *I respect those differences, I respect their uniqueness.*
> *I wish happiness, peace, and the blessings of life to all*

Bottom Line:
With a strong connection to the spirit, all things change.

You now can experience "joie de vivre". You glow and people glow around you too! Your positive attitude, and bubbly energy allow your life to be magical!

Don't ask me how this happens—I really couldn't tell you. But it does, trust me!

I'm in my 60s and my doctor just read my blood work and told me that I am as healthy as a 20-year-old. "Joie de vivre" keeps you young! Victory to me.

And If I can, YOU CAN too!

Get ready for it! Victory is yours!

FOOD FOR THOUGHT

*"Without leaps of imagination, or dreaming,
we lose the excitement of possibilities. Dreaming, after all,
is a form of planning."*

-GLORIA STEINEM

*"Trust yourself. Create the kind of self that you will be happy
to live with all of your life. Make the most of yourself by
fanning the tiny, inner sparks of possibility
into flames of achievement."*

-GOLDA MEIR

Chapter 10

Final Words

Meditation to Inspire You on the Journey

"The Night Walk"

TO DEVELOP INTUITION

Sit comfortably and breathe deeply.

It's a peaceful, moonlit night. You are calm. You are walking on a dirt road, deep in the country, moonlit fields on either side. A gentle breeze blows through your hair. The smell of summer flowers stirs your senses; the wind awakens the fields, animating the tall grass. The mating songs of cicadas fills the air. You are completely safe in the darkness of night.

Stop for a moment and look up to the starry sky. Let your mind seek its furthest places. Transport yourself to the deepest space.

This is an excellent time to ask for guidance from some higher power, from some force which is both in you and beyond you. Be sensitive to all possible answers (verbal, visual, intuitive). Such answers may come now or may come later as you begin to interpret this night's journey into the starry sky. Listen!

THINK TO YOURSELF:

*My intuition illuminates my path I am led towards my vision.
I am grateful for such guidance.*

Know now that your intuition is always with you. It is always there awaiting your return. Return to the night sky.

Final Thoughts

There you have it, dear friend— your toolkit, all the techniques you need to begin your practice of life change. Use them, practice them, engage yourself fully in them... for these are the techniques which will maintain your life's house clean and tidy, and keep it in the best possible condition.

As you continue along your path of change, you will gain faith in your new abilities. You realize that you have freedom of choice, and you are no longer bound by limiting patterns of behavior. The challenges that come your way no longer frighten you—instead they excite you because you know that they provide the opportunity for greater life victories! Remember, you have acquired a new conditioning and because of that, you surprise yourself by thinking and acting in productive ways. Victories come frequently, so often that you come to the unmistakable conclusion that you are the victor of your own life!

I want to share one last story with you that will inspire you on your journey!

In final preparation for their lives as Buddhist monks, the Dali Lama has his novices engage in a challenging initiation ceremony. They are asked to enter a room where they will face all their fears, doubts, anxieties, and wrestle their demons... They are told that they need to pass through that room to the single door on the other side which leads them beyond the disturbances of the human mind. Their success depends on keeping their focus on the door which leads to the light...

This rite of passage is powerful, for with it, such monks fully establish for themselves the fact that they have moved beyond the delusions of the human mind—the illusions which condemn them to a life of human suffering.

So, my dear friend, never forget this story and promise yourself that no matter what happens in your life, to keep your eye on the exit door, on your desired outcome, on your success!

And before it's time to say goodbye, I want to present you with two important documents for your lifelong journey! a summary of **the Fresh Start Program** that I suggest using every day and then the **Fresh Start Contract**. Remember, the one at the beginning of the book? Ok? One final contract... Think of it as sending out a message to your**self,** that you are committed to lifelong change, to a life filled with compassion, wonder, honesty and "joie de vivre". VICTORY!

VICTIM TO VICTORIOUS

DAILY GUIDE FOR YOUR VICTORIOUS LIFE

- Greet every day with a smile on your face to welcome new opportunities.
- Put on your armor of light for protection against negativity and carry the sword of fearlessness for courage and strength.
- Walk with confidence, your lungs filled with air, your head touching the sky and your feet kissing the earth.
- Remember to stay calm, centered and feel connected to the power of universal energy.
- Welcome every challenge as an opportunity to test your courage and to develop your strength of character.
- Stay focused on what you desire to change, and not on what has happened in the past, which cannot be changed.
- Ask yourself what you are learning from this situation, instead of why this situation has happened to you.
- Change your attitude and behavior to achieve different results.
- Look for a clear intention before you decide to take any action.
- Do not wait for a miracle, create one.
- Do not search for perfection, accept being human.
- Affirm and repeat every day: I CAN, I DO, I WILL. VICTORY IS MINE!

VICTIM TO VICTORIOUS

LIFELONG VICTORY CONTRACT

Once again and forever more, I declare:

- I am a unique individual, with a special purpose.
- I am meant to have a rich and fulfilling life.
- I am worthy of respect and self-respect.
- I have within myself gifts, talents, strengths, and unrealized potential.
- I create unconditional love and acceptance for myself.
- I choose a kind and caring attitude towards others.
- I make my dreams a reality.

Therefore, I commit to...

- Use my daily practices on my journey to greater life growth.
- Continue my practice of being kind and loving towards myself and others.
- Continue to look within for divine intelligence and guidance.
- Continue to view every challenge as an opportunity to further my dream.
- Continue to discard outdated, counterproductive, and anxiety-producing ways of thinking.
- Continue to use the *3C's* and the *Screening Room* to further advance my life change.
- Continue to use the *language of the heart* to create loving connections to yourself and others.
- Continue to use my *mindful eating* practices so that I experience health and vibrant energy.
- Continue to grow my connection to the spirit to express compassion.

VICTIM TO VICTORIOUS

- Develop my intuition and "joie de vivre".
- Forge ahead to greater life victories.
- Continue to trust and believe that my life has purpose and significance.
- I will pursue my goals with clear intention and honesty. I am willing to continue to do the work required to transform my attitude and my life. Nothing and no one can stop me from manifesting my vision of the person I desire to be.

VICTORY TO ME!

_____   _____

(sign)   Date

VICTIM TO VICTORIOUS

Index of Practices

The Rowboat Meditation..page 23

Square breathing practice ....page 25

3C's Mindfulness Meditation practice...........................page 27

Mindful walk practice...page 29

Mindful eating practice..page 31

The lighthouse Meditation..page 38

Dexxtra practice..page 41

The Sword of light Meditation.......................................page 51

Armor of the light Meditation.......................................page 57

The horizon Meditation..page 61

Screening room practice...page 65

The garden of the heart Meditation ....page 68

The Satellite Meditation...page 83

The night walk Meditation..page 87

About Edwige Gilbert

A native of Cannes, France, Edwige Gilbert is the Author of *"The Fresh Start Promise: 28 Days to Total Mind, Body, and Spirit Transformation"*. She is *a* stress management Coach as well as the founder of New Life Directions. For over 30 years she has worked with individuals and groups, conducting seminars, retreats and lectures around the world. *Her forte is teaching people how to turn Stress into Strength, clear unwanted habits, and live healthier and happier lives with Joie de vivre.* She currently offers an Online course at GenconnectU.com entitled *"How to handle stress for a joyful and balanced life"*.

She has been featured on **Lifetime TV** ("The Balancing Act") on national radio and in such magazines as **New York Magazine, Personal Excellence,** *Woman's World, American Health, Allure,* **and Women's Fitness**. Edwige holds certifications in Neuro-Linguistic Programming (N.L.P) Hypnotherapy, Substance abuse counseling, Behavioral change, Yoga, Mindfulness Meditation practice and Qigong. Some of her clients include, MTV, Citigroup, the Corcoran Group, Expedia, Pritikin weight loss center and the Alzheimer's Association among others.

To contact Edwige Check out her website

newlifedirections.com

Or E mail her at edwige@newlifedirections.com

www.ingramcontent.com/pod-product-compliance
Lightning Source LLC
LaVergne TN
LVHW050625090426
835512LV00007B/669